Explore new ideas!

Welcome to your Reading/Writing Workshop

Read exciting literature, science and social studies texts!

Become an expert writer!

Build vocabulary and knowledge to unlock the Wonders of reading!

Use your student login to explore your interactive Reading/Writing Workshop, practice close reading, and more.

Go Digital! www.connected.mcgraw-hill.com

Cover and Title pages: Nathan Love

www.mheonline.com/readingwonders

Send all inquiries to:
McGraw-Hill Education
2 Penn Plaza
New York, NY 10121

ISBN: 978-0-07-679764-6
MHID: 0-07-679764-3

Printed in the United States of America.

6 7 8 9 LWI 20 19 18

Program Authors

Diane August	Jan Hasbrouck
Donald R. Bear	Margaret Kilgo
Janice A. Dole	Jay McTighe
Jana Echevarria	Scott G. Paris
Douglas Fisher	Timothy Shanahan
David Francis	Josefina V. Tinajero
Vicki Gibson	

Mc
Graw
Hill
Education

Unit 3

Changes Over Time

The Big Idea

What can happen over time? 6

Go Digital! www.connected.mcgraw-hill.com

SOCIAL STUDIES

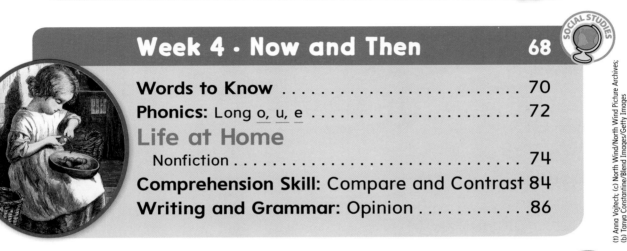

The Big Idea

What can happen over time?

Changes Over Time

Changes, Changes

Little by little, day by day,
Things grow and change in
every way.

Trees get taller and touch the sky,
Eggs hatch new birds who
learn to fly.

A puppy born in spring is small,
But he'll be bigger when it's fall.

I'm also growing, bit by bit,
Just see—my clothes no
longer fit!

—by George Samos

Cathy Delanssay

Essential Question

How do we measure time?

Go Digital!

COLLABORATE

Talk About It

What are these children learning to do?

Ariel Skelley/Blend Images/Corbis

8

All About Time

away

Do all birds fly **away** in fall?

now

It's time for us to eat **now**.

some

Some kids like to wear a watch.

today

It is my birthday **today**!

way

A clock is one **way** to tell time.

why

Why is summer a fun season?

COLLABORATE

Your Turn

Say the sentence for each word. Then make up another sentence.

Go Digital! Use the online visual glossary

(tl) Sean Duan/Flickr/Getty Images; (cl) BlueMoon Stock/Alamy; (bl) Shiyana Thenabadu/Alamy; (tr) UpperCut Images/Alamy; (cr) Comstock Images; (br) Fuse/Getty Images

Long a

The a_e spelling makes the long a sound in **wake**.

date	whale	shakes
wave	safe	plate
snake	game	grapes
trades	vase	brave

Dave gave Jane a plate of grapes.

Can the ants take the grapes?

Your Turn

Look for these words with long a spelled a_e in "Nate the Snake Is Late."

Nate	snake	late	make
wade	lake	wake	gaze
lane	gate	Tate	

Genre Fantasy

Essential Question

How do we measure time?

Read about how Nate the snake keeps track of time.

Go Digital!

Kenneth Spengler

14

Nate the Snake Is Late

It is 8 o'clock, and I can not be late.

I do not wish to make my pals wait.

I must be there at half past ten.

But I have lots of time until then.

Kenneth Spengler

At last I am set and on my **way** there,

But I think I still have **some** time to spare.

I wade in this lake as frogs
hop **away**.

I do not think they wish to play!

Kenneth Spengler

The sun is hot, and I nap on a rock.

Then I wake up and gaze at the clock.

20

Drats! It is 10 o'clock. Can it be?

Will my pals still be there for me?

I dash up a lane and past the gate.

I am on my way, but am I late?

My six best pals sit with Miss Tate.

I tell them all **why** I am late.

They grin at me and then they say,
"**Now** we can hear the story **today**!"

23

Character, Setting, Plot

A **character** is a person or an animal in a story. The **setting** is where and when a story takes place.

The **plot** of a story is what happens at the beginning, middle, and end.

🔍 Find Text Evidence

Find out what happens at the beginning of the story.

page 16

It is 8 o'clock, and I can not be late.

I do not wish to make my pals wait.

Kenneth Spengler

Beginning

Nate wakes up at 8 o'clock.
He does not want to be late.

Middle

Nate does many things, such as wade in
the lake. Then he takes a nap.

End

Nate gets to the library late for story
hour. But his friends wait for him.

Your Turn

COLLABORATE

Talk about the plot of "Nate the
Snake Is Late."

Go Digital! *Use the interactive graphic organizer*

Write About the Text

Pages 14–23

Luke

I responded to the prompt: **Add two pages between pages 17–18. What does Nate do to get ready?**

Student Model: *Narrative Text*

I have time to grab something to eat. A juicy, red apple is a yummy treat!

Grammar

The word **grab** is a **verb**, or action word.

Sensory Details

I used the words **juicy** and **red** to tell about the apple.

I need my cap.
Oh, where could it be?
I look by my bed.
There it is, I see!

Rhyming Words
I ended my lines with the words <u>be</u> and <u>see</u>.

Your Turn

Add two pages to "Nate the Snake Is Late" telling what happens next. Write rhyming sentences like the story.

Go Digital!
Write your response online.
Use your editing checklist.

Essential Question

How do plants change as they grow?

Go Digital!

COLLABORATE

Talk About It

What does the boy see growing? How will it change?

Ready, Set, Grow!

green

Peas and beans are **green**.

grow

Plants get big when they **grow**.

pretty

The flowers are **pretty** colors.

should

Which seeds **should** I plant?

together

Together we can pull the weeds.

water

Water comes out of the hose.

Your Turn

COLLABORATE

Say the sentence for each word.
Then make up another sentence.

Go Digital! **Use the online visual glossary**

(tl) Goodshoot/Alamy; (cl) Image Source/Alamy; (bl) FogStock/Alamy; (tr) Pixtal/age fotostock; (cr) Ariel Skelley/Blend Images/Getty Images; (br) Huntstock/the Agency Collection/Getty Images

Long i

The i_e spelling makes the long i sound, as in **bite**.

likes	white	five
whines	wide	size
ripe	hide	time
drives	prize	shine

Dan Andreasen

32

Five fine pumpkins are on a vine.

What size is the prize pumpkin?

COLLABORATE

Your Turn

Look for these words with long i spelled i_e in "Time to Plant!"

time	Mike	White	fine	five
shines	vines	like	while	
bite	ripe	piles	yikes	

33

Essential Question

How do plants change as they grow?

Read about how vegetable plants grow.

Go Digital!

34

Dan Andreasen

Time to Plant!

Cast

Beth

Mike

Gramps

Dad

Mom

Miss White

Narrator

Beth: Dad, can we plant a garden?

Dad: Yes! That will be fine!

Gramps: We can plant vegetables.

Mike: Yum! Let's do it **together**.

Mom:	Dad and I will dig.
Mike:	I will drop in five seeds.
Gramps:	I will set in **green** plants.
Beth:	And I will get **water**!

Narrator: Days pass. The sun shines. Rain plinks and plunks.

Beth: I can spot buds on the vines!

Dad: Sun and water made them **grow**.

Narrator: Days pass. The sun shines. Rain drips and drops.

Beth: The vegetables got big!

Dad: We **should** pick them.

Mom: Yes, it's time!

Dan Andreasen

Mike: I like to munch while I pick. I will take a bite. Yum!

Gramps: Sun and water made them ripe.

Narrator: They pick piles and piles.

Beth: Yikes! That's a lot!

Mike: We can't eat them all.

Gramps: I think I have a plan.

Dan Andreasen

Mike: This bag is for you.

Miss White: They are such **pretty** vegetables! Thank you!

Beth: Sun and water made them grow.

Sequence

Events in a story or a play happen in a certain order, or **sequence**. The events are the plot of the story.

 Find Text Evidence

Find the first thing that happens in "Time to Plant!"

page 37

Beth:	Dad, can we plant a garden?
Dad:	Yes! That will be fine!
Gramps:	We can plant vegetables.
Mike:	Yum! Let's do it **together**.

Dan Andreasen

44

First

The family plants a garden.

Next

The plants get big and grow.

Then

The family picks the vegetables.

Last

They share their vegetables.

COLLABORATE

Your Turn

Talk about the plot of "Time to Plant!"

Go Digital! *Use the interactive graphic organizer*

Pages 34–43

Write About the Text

Elizabeth

I responded to the prompt: **Write more lines for the end of the play. Tell what Miss White says.**

Character
I wrote Miss White's name to tell the words that she says.

Student Model: *Narrative Text*

Miss White: Thank you! These vegetables look ripe and delicious. Will all of you join me for dinner? I can use the tomatoes to make a special soup.

Specific Words
I used specific words, such as <u>tomatoes</u> instead of <u>vegetables</u>.

Then I can slice the beans for a fine dish. I can add some fresh peas to our plates! I like fresh peas. It is fun to share a meal with friends!

Grammar
The **verb** <u>like</u> is in the present tense.

Your Turn

Add a page to the end of the story in which the kids tell Miss White what they did to grow the plants.

Go Digital!
Write your response online.
Use your editing checklist.

Essential Question

What is a folktale?

Go Digital!

48

Story Time

Talk About It

What are these children acting out?

any

Do you have **any** fairy tales?

from

Gram read to us **from** her book.

happy

I am **happy** to be in the play.

once

Once upon a time there was a queen.

so

That story is **so** funny!

upon

Once **upon** a time there was a king.

Your Turn

COLLABORATE

Say the sentence for each word. Then make up another sentence.

Go Digital! **Use the online visual glossary**

(tl) Shalom Ormsby/Blend Images/Getty Images; (cl) Jakob Helbig/Digital Vision/Getty Images; (bl) Dirk Anschutz/Stone/Getty Images; (tr) Matthieu Spohn/ PhotoAlto Agency RF Collections/Getty Images; (cr) REB Images/Blend Images/Getty Images; (br) Brand New Images/Stone/Getty Images

Soft c and Soft g

The letter c can make the soft c sound you hear in **race**.

The letters g and dge can make the soft g sound you hear in **age** and **edge**.

face	place	space
nice	slices	cents
page	cage	stage
pledge	fudge	gem

Anna Vojtech

Madge eats a big slice of fudge.

Gen likes to sing on a stage.

Your Turn

Look for these words with soft c and soft g in "The Nice Mitten."

nice	Lance	edge
mice	place	raced
hedgehog	space	trace

53

Essential Question

What is a folktale?

Read the story of a little boy's lost mitten.

Go Digital!

Anna Vojtech

54

The Nice Mitten

Once upon a time, a boy named
Lance went out to pick up sticks.
His mom gave him nice red
mittens in case his hands got cold.

Anna Vojtech

"Take the mittens and keep them safe," his mom said. But as Lance left, he ran fast and lost a mitten at the edge of the wide forest.

Five mice saw the mitten. "This is a nice place to rest," they said. **So** the **happy** mice went in and rested.

Then, a rabbit raced by. "This is
a nice place for hiding," she said.
So the rabbit went in and hid.
The mitten puffed up a bit.

Next, a hedgehog came sniffing
by. "This is a nice place for taking
a nap," he said. So the hedgehog
went in and slept. The mitten
puffed up a bit more.

Just then, a big bear came by.
"This is a nice place to get warm,"
he said. So the big bear went in.
The mitten puffed up **from** all
the animals in it. It puffed up as
much as a mitten can.

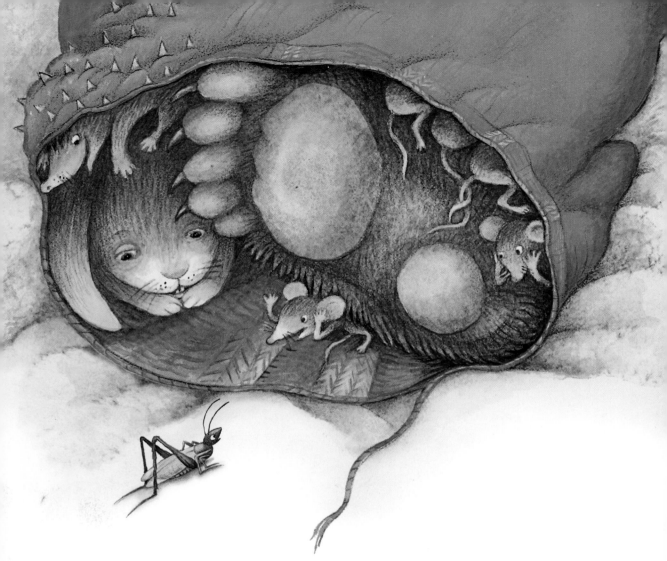

At last, a black cricket came by. "This is a nice place," he said.

"We do not have **any** space," said the animals in the mitten.

But the black cricket went in. And just as he did...

Rip! Snap! POP!

When Lance came back, there
was not a trace of red mitten left.
So sad!

Cause and Effect

A **cause** is what makes something happen in a story.

An **effect** is the event that happens.

To find the cause and the effect, ask: What happened? Why did it happen?

 Find Text Evidence

Find the causes and effects in the story.

page 57

"Take the mittens and keep them safe," his mom said. But as Lance left, he ran fast and lost a mitten at the edge of the wide forest.

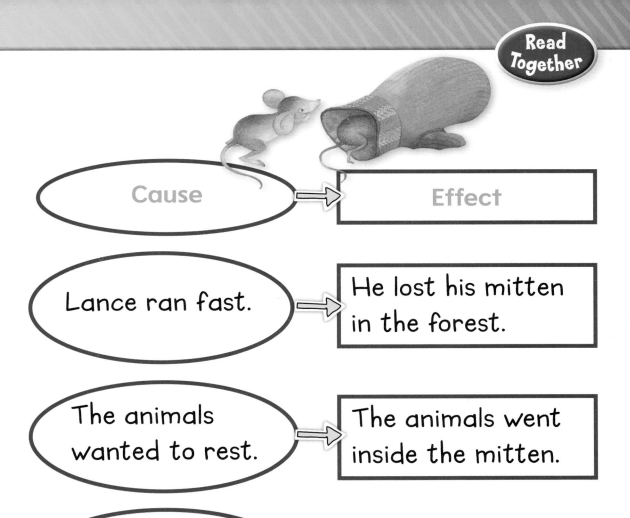

Cause		Effect
Lance ran fast.	→	He lost his mitten in the forest.
The animals wanted to rest.	→	The animals went inside the mitten.
Too many animals went in.	→	The mitten puffed up and got too big.

Your Turn

COLLABORATE

Talk about the cause and effect of story events in "The Nice Mitten."

Go Digital! *Use the interactive graphic organizer*

65

Write About the Text

Pages 54–63

Anna

I responded to the prompt: **Rewrite the story with a lost boot instead of a lost mitten.**

Student Model: *Narrative Text*

Once upon a time, Lance hiked to the river for water. On the way, he lost his boot in the sticky mud.

A wet mouse hid in his boot to dry off. Then, a bird flew in. Next, a fox crawled inside.

Strong Verbs
I used **strong verbs** such as <u>hiked</u>, <u>flew</u>, and <u>crawled</u> to make the story exciting.

Sequence
I told events in a sequence that made sense.

Lance came back from the river. He found his boot in the mud. He shook it out, and all of the animals fell out.

The animals followed Lance home, and they all lived happily ever after.

Grammar

Verb endings like **-ed** tell about action in the **past.**

COLLABORATE

Your Turn

Rewrite the story so that the boy loses a jacket, sock, or hat instead of a mitten.

Go Digital!
Write your response online.
Use your editing checklist.

67

Essential Question

How is life different than it was long ago?

Go Digital!

Once Upon a Time

Talk About It

What are the children playing? Tell how they are like or different than you.

ago

Schools were small long **ago**.

boy

That **boy** likes to skate.

girl

This **girl** can ride a bike well.

how

How did kids play in the past?

old

Old homes were made of logs.

people

People went by horse and buggy.

Your Turn

Say the sentence for each word. Then make up another sentence.

Go Digital! **Use the online visual glossary**

(tl) Bear Dancer Studios/Mark Dierker; (cl) Jupiterimages/Comstock Images/Getty Images; (bl) Don Mason/Blend Images LLC; (tr) Constance Bannister Corp/Archive Photos/Getty Images; (cr) IS2 from Image Source/Alamy; (br) Design Pics/Carson Ganci

Long o, u, e

The o_e spelling makes the long o sound in **phone**.

The u_e spelling makes the long u sound in **use**.

The e_e spelling makes the long e sound in **these**.

bone	**cute**	**Eve**
drove	**hoped**	**these**
Steve	**mule**	**stone**
broke	**voted**	**cubes**

Valeria Cis

72

Can Pete use this phone?

Zeke is Rose's cute mule.

Your Turn

COLLABORATE

Look for these words with o_e, u_e, and e_e in "Life at Home."

home	homes	pole
huge	use	stove
these	those	

73

Essential Question

How is life different than it was long ago?

Read about how life at home is different today than it was long ago.

Go Digital!

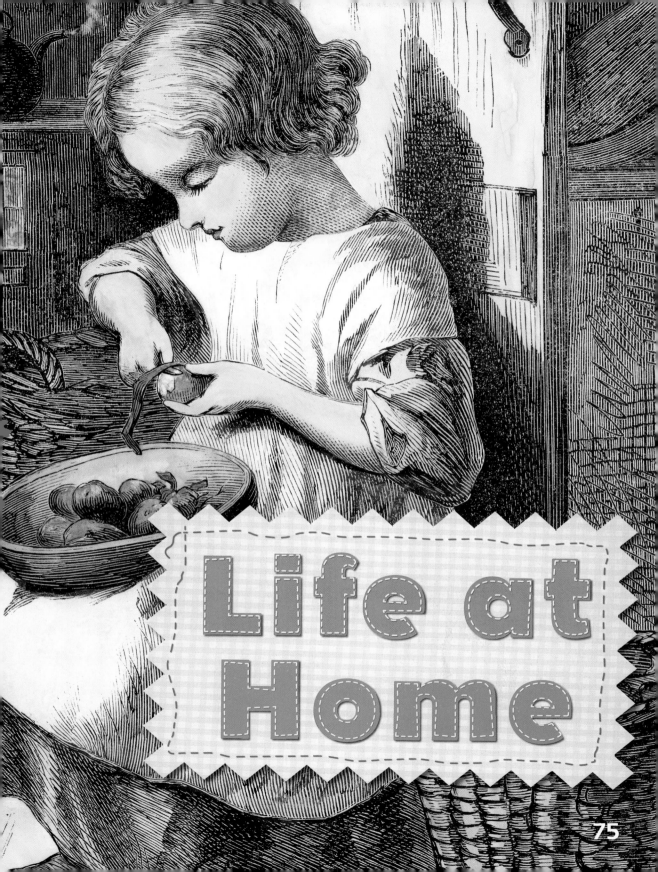

Life at Home

Has home life changed a lot since long **ago**?

Yes, it has!

Long ago, many families cooked worked, and slept in one room.

Today, families can live in large homes that have lots of space.

A long time ago, homes had just one room. **People** ate and slept in that same room.

Today, homes can have many rooms.

How did people cook and bake long ago?

A home had a brick fireplace with a pole. A huge pot hung on this pole. People cooked in this big pot.

Long ago, there was an oven at the side of the fireplace. Bread was baked there.

Today, stoves can use
gas or electricity.

Now, we use a stove
to cook and bake things.
We still use pots.
But these pots are not
as big as that **old** pot!

Back then, kids helped out a lot.
A **boy** helped his dad plant crops.
A **girl** helped her mom inside the
home. She made socks and caps.
It takes a long time to make those
things.

A spinning wheel was used to spin wool into yarn.

Today, people buy most of the things they need and want.

Now, we shop for things such as socks and caps. We shop for things to eat, as well.

But kids still help out at home.

Back then, people got water from a well. Then they filled up a big tub and washed things.

In the past, people washed dishes in a tub made of wood.

Now, people can wash things in a sink. We can wash dishes in a dishwasher, too.

Life is not as hard today as it was long ago!

Today, it's easy to wash dishes in a sink or dishwasher.

Hero Images/Digital Vision/Getty Images

Compare and Contrast

When you compare, you think about how things are alike.

When you contrast, you think about how things are different.

 Find Text Evidence

Find out how homes long ago and today are alike and different.

page 77

A long time ago, homes had just one room. **People** ate and slept in that same room.

Today, homes can have many rooms.

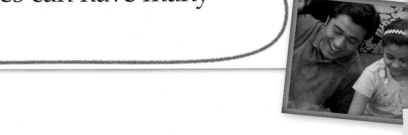

Long Ago

Homes had one room.

Both

People live in homes.

Now

Homes have many rooms.

COLLABORATE

Your Turn

Talk about how home life is alike and different in "Life at Home."

Go Digital! Use the interactive graphic organizer

Write About the Text

Pages 74–83

Mateo

I answered the question: **Would you rather cook as we do now or as people did long ago? Why?**

Student Model: *Opinion*

I read "Life at Home" and I would rather cook as we do now. Long ago, people cooked over a big fire. They used one big pot. They could only make one thing at a time.

Topic
I named the selection and what I wrote about.

Reasons
I gave a reason for my opinion.

Now we use a stove to cook. We can cook many things because the stove is able to fit many pots. I like that cooking now is easier. You can make many foods at the same time.

Grammar
The **verb** **is** tells about one thing.

Your Turn COLLABORATE

Based on "Life at Home," do you think home life is better now, or was it better in the past? Why?

Go Digital!
Write your response online.
Use your editing checklist.

North Wind Picture Archives

87

Weekly Concept From Farm to Table

Essential Question
How do we get our food?

Go Digital!

dpa picture alliance archive/Alamy Stock Photo

Food's Journey

COLLABORATE

Talk About It
What happens to farm goods before you eat them?

after

Bread has a crust **after** it is baked.

buy

They **buy** oranges at the store.

done

They are **done** and ready to eat.

every

Every grape is plump and purple.

soon

They will go to the store **soon**.

work

Machines help do the **work**.

Your Turn

Say the sentence for each word. Then make up another sentence.

Go Digital! **Use the online visual glossary**

oo, u

The letters oo and u can make the sound you hear in the middle of **good** and **push**.

cook	looking	pull
hood	foot	took
hooked	books	wool
put	stood	shook

Jake put on his wool coat.

He will pull up the hood.

Your Turn

COLLABORATE

Look for these words with oo and u in "A Look at Breakfast."

look   good   put

full   cooked   pulled

Essential Question

How do we get our food?

Read about where breakfast foods come from.

Go Digital!

A Look at Breakfast

Bread is good for breakfast. But this isn't bread yet. It is wheat. Flour will be made from the wheat.

The wheat is crushed to make flour.

Bloomberg via Getty Images

First, dough is made. Next, the dough is shaped and baked. Then, it is **done**. It is bread. Last, the bread is put in bags.

Grape jam is good on bread. But this isn't jam yet. It is a grape vine full of grapes.

Grapes grow on vines and then are picked when they are ripe.

Alberto Nardi/AGF RM/age fotostock

Trucks take the grapes to a plant. **Every** grape is crushed to make mush. **After** that, the mush is cooked. Now, it is grape jam. Yum!

Orange juice is good for breakfast, too! Lots and lots of sun makes oranges big and ripe. They will taste good. **Soon**, the big, ripe oranges will get pulled down.

Trucks take piles and piles of oranges to a plant. Then, they get washed. Next, they get crushed. Big sacks get filled with juice.

The food is shipped in trucks to shops. It is stacked up. Now, it is for sale. People will **buy** it and bring it home. It will make a good breakfast!

It takes **work** to make food for breakfast.

Food	Where It Comes From	How It Is Made
bread	wheat	Wheat is crushed into flour. Dough is made. Dough is baked into bread.
grape jam	grapes	Grapes are crushed to make mush. Mush is cooked into jam.
orange juice	oranges	Oranges are crushed into juice.

Sequence

Authors often give information in **sequence**, or time order. Words such as **first, next, then,** and **last** help you understand the sequence.

🔍 Find Text Evidence

Find the first thing that happens when flour is made into bread.

page 97

First, dough is made. Next, the dough is shaped and baked. Then, it is **done**. It is bread. Last, the bread is put in bags.

First

Dough is made.

⬇

Next

The dough is shaped and baked.

⬇

Then

It is done.

⬇

Last

The bread is put in bags.

Your Turn

Talk about how other foods in "A Look at Breakfast" are made. Tell what happens in sequence.

Go Digital! **Use the interactive graphic organizer**

105

Write About the Text

Pages 94–103

Lisa

I answered the question: **Which breakfast item do you think is the hardest to make? Why?**

Student Model: *Opinion*

Reasons
I gave a reason for my opinion.

I think bread is the hardest breakfast food to make. It takes many steps to make it.

First, the farmer grows wheat. Then, wheat is crushed into flour.

Next, the flour is mixed to make dough. Last, the dough is shaped into loaves and baked.

It takes more steps to make bread than jam or juice. It isn't easy to make bread.

Tanya Constantine/Blend Images/Getty Images